The WEDDING of a POET

A ONE-ACT COMEDY (1859)

İBRAHIM ŞINASI

TRANSLATED FROM THE TURKISH BY

EDWARD ALLWORTH

GRIFFON HOUSE PUBLICATIONS

P.O. Box 81 • Whitestone, New York 11357

Sinasi, Ibrahim, 1826-1871.
   The wedding of a poet.

   Translation of Sair evlenmesi.
   At head of title: The first modern Turkish play.
   I. Title.
PL248.S52S213   1981   894'.3523   81-6855
ISBN 0-918680-15-8   AACR2

COVER DESIGN BY JOAN ATTURA

THE WEDDING OF A POET

ACKNOWLEDGEMENTS

The translator would like to thank Mrs. Adalet Avanoğlu, Dr. Ahmet O. Evin, and Ambassador Talat Sait Halman for their generous advice during the preparation of the manuscript. The final draft has greatly benefited from the careful stage reading and theatrical know-how of Dr. Nishan Parlakian and sensitive editing by Dr. Anne Paolucci—and I am especially grateful for their suggestions.

The music included here was transcribed from the original by Miss Janna Saslaw.

The present translation was made from the Turkish text published in Tercümen-i Ahval *(numbers 2-5, October-November 1860) and in the Remzi Kitabevi edition issued in Istanbul (1958).*

The photographs of nineteenth-century Turkish costumes were prepared by Mr. Manny Warman from Osman Hamdi Bey, Les costumes populaires de la Turquie en 1873 *(Constantinople: Commission Imperiale Ottomane pur l'Exposition Universelle de Vienne; Imprimerie du "Levant Times & Shipping Gazette," 1873), Plates I, II, and IV.*

E.A.

CONTENTS

PREFACE

PLAYWRIGHT AND PLAY. *İbrahim Şinasi (1826-1871) became the first modern Turkish playwright only after the mid-nineteenth century. By then, Istanbul had already enjoyed for a long time both folk theatricals in the country's primary language and foreign performances of dramas in the European languages. But, with* Wedding of a Poet, *Şinasi offered, for the first time, an indigenous stage piece in a European style—writing it in ordinary Turkish, rather than in the usual bookish medium of standard literature. And, equally important, he treated a contemporary subject in an up-to-date fashion. Şinasi knew the traditional language perfectly, for he had returned from some four years' study in Paris about 1853 to take up an active life in Turkey. He wrote conventional odes, translated from French poets, worked as editor and publisher of the newspaper* Tasvir-i Efkâr, *and wrote for other papers as well. At the same time, he served as a member of the Board of Education.*

THE WEDDING OF A POET (SAIR EVLENMESI). *Written in 1859, the play was published in installments in* Tercümen-i Ahval *(1860). Each segment was labeled* Tefriqa *(feuilleton / serial)—the word which is reproduced, in the Arabic script, on the back cover. The play came out in Ottoman Turkey under circumstances resembling those that created the earliest modern theater and plays throughout the Middle East between 1840 and 1870. The combination of visiting troupes from Europe—as well as sojourns in London, Paris, St. Petersburg or Vienna—and a strong foreign presence in several parts of the region gave impetus to new drama. Essential, also, seemed to be some innovation in urban education, which began to nourish modern stage life in cultural centers such as Tbilisi (Tiflis), Beirut, Istanbul, and Cairo.*

In the Turkish case, Şinasi's initiative with this comedy was followed not by his own dramatic works—for there were none, evidently—but by those of ensuing decades of Ottoman playwrights. The Wedding of a Poet *deals with the fortunes of a specific hack writer as he enters the marriage market, rather than with generalizations about poets and their married life in the Middle East, around the 1800s. The play purports to show* the impatience of the new men with old practices, satirizing go-betweens and arranged marriages. But it also chides the emerging, self-styled intellectuals and poets for their pontificating about "thiyator," artistic pretensions among the ghosts of a towering literary heritage, and pseudo-liberalism coupled with snobbery toward the less educated. Şinasi's nine brief scenes spoof the ridiculous side of the ways of town-folk, but at the same time offer popular humor in the most amusing kind of dialogue. Altogether, this sophisticated first effort out of a strong literary environment and age had a lasting and subtle value.

There is no known previous translation of the play into English.

TRANSLATOR. *Edward Allworth lectures on Middle East drama and theater at Columbia University, Department of Middle East Languages and Culture. Other publications by Professor Allworth in this field include: "The Beginnings of the Modern Turkestanian Theater,"* Slavic Review *4 (1964); "Reform and Revolution in Early Uzbek Drama,"* Central Asian Review *2 (1964); "Murder as Metaphor in the First Central Asian Drama,"* Edebiyat. A Journal of Middle Eastern Literature *Vol. IV, No. 1 (1979 [in process]); "Introduction to Modern Drama of the Transcaucasus," in* Evil Spirit (Char Voki) *by Alexandre Shirvanzade, translated by Nishan Parlakian (New York, St. Vartan Press, 1980); "Drama and Theater of the Russian East: Transcaucasus, Tatarstan, Central Asia,"* Bibliographical Anthology of Theatrical Movement, *edited by Robert Fleshman and Diane Carney (New Orleans, Loyola University [in process]).*

THE WEDDING OF A POET

CAST OF CHARACTERS

Mr. Ardent-Hack　　　*Bridegroom, Miss Dove's Adorer (a versifier)*

Master Wise　　　*Mr. Ardent-Hack's close friend*

Miss Dove　　　*Beloved of Mr. Ardent-Hack, and Miss Placid's younger sister (tall and slim)*

Miss Placid　　　*Betrothed to Mr. Ardent-Hack (short and stocky, in her forties)*

Dame Belle　　　*Matchmaker*

Mrs. Acne　　　*Matron of Honor*

Reverend Gobbledegook　　　*Minor clerical official who arranged Miss Placid's marriage contract*

Officer Boggywits　　　*Precinct patrolman*

Red Sparsewhisker　　　*Precinct street cleaner*

Neighborhood Crowd　　　*Local shopkeepers, handcraftsmen, and peddlers*

The scene is Mr. Ardent-Hack's parlor, the day of his wedding.

I.
MIDDLE-CLASS MEN OF CONSTANTINOPLE. The one on the left is in the Europeanized costume of the day; the one on the right wears the traditional dress. In the center, a servant (*ayvaz*).

II.
THREE WORKING MEN. From Left to Right: a water-carrier
(*saka*); porter or general carrier (*hamal*); boatman (*kayikci*).

MR. ARDENT-HACK

At last, this evening I become a bridegroom. Luckily, I signed the marriage contract today. If I hadn't, passion and excitement might have made me an unwed bridegroom!

MASTER WISE

Is such a thing possible?

MR. ARDENT-HACK

Why not, if it's a love match—as they say.

MASTER WISE

Shocking!

MR. ARDENT-HACK

(Quickly) Now, see here, if a husband can get along without passion or affection, fine for him! But what am I marrying Miss Dove for? Because . . . because . . . she's my *darling*, and nothing else! Wasn't I *sane* to fall in love with her so *madly*?

MASTER WISE

Maybe so . . . .

MR. ARDENT-HACK

Ah, the freshness of her beauty . . . the sweetness of her disposition! Everything about her pleases me. (Sigh) Now, if my poor Dove just did not have a big sister with a face like a crow—

MASTER WISE

Oh! A shame! What do they call her?

MR. ARDENT-HACK

Uh, Miss Placid, I believe. Even the name of the wretched woman bothers me.

MASTER WISE

Why is that?

MR. ARDENT-HACK

When it comes to good looks, she's. . . *destitute.* But, forget about that. Besides staying out of circulation until forty-five, her brains have gone bankrupt too. I guess there's nothing to her except an over-inflated hulk. (Sigh) I'm ashamed to be seen with such a sister-in-law!

MASTER WISE

What can you do? When you love the rose, you put up with its thorns. Watch they don't play a trick on you and switch *her* for Miss Dove! That's the way of the world! People don't usually marry off a young daughter while an old one stays at home, you know.

MR. ARDENT-HACK

Now look, Master Wise! I don't mind jokes. But there's a limit.

MASTER WISE

Then why are *you* jokingly offering her to me, eh?

MR. ARDENT-HACK

You think I'm trying to be funny? I'm serious about arranging things for you, my friend!

MASTER WISE

A lame excuse is worse than none.

MR. ARDENT-HACK

I'm not trying to apologize for myself.

MASTER WISE

Excuse me!

MR. ARDENT-HACK

Oh, shut up! Here comes Dame Belle, my matchmaker. They're bringing my dear Dovie. Go sit in the living room. We'll get together later on.

SECOND SCENE   *MR. ARDENT-HACK, DAME BELLE*

DAME BELLE

Good news, Ardent-Hack my boy, good news! Here comes the bride. She's on the way.

MR. ARDENT-HACK

(Sigh) Most esteemed Mother! Would I ever really have attained my heart's desire without you? What can I do in return? I don't know!

DAME BELLE

My Son! Why have I remained on this perfidious earth, if not to arrange such auspicious affairs? Now that I have survived to see this happy occasion, truly, why should I live any longer? I don't want to . . . don't want to. But, before .my eyes are closed for good, let me see your sons just once . . . with long white beards!

MR. ARDENT-HACK

You've made my wish come true—so, as long as you live, Madam, Viva! (Begins jumping and dancing for joy)

DAME BELLE

Oh, my lamb, you'd better calm down! Don't forget, you entered into a solemn marriage contract. Be a trifle more dignified!

MR. ARDENT-HACK

Should a man act downhearted at his own wedding? Just the opposite! Anyway, go ahead, go ahead, please! Stand outside and wait for the young lade! Let me practice being dignified here by myself for a while.

THIRD SCENE   *MR. ARDENT-HACK (ALONE)*

Now, my lovie Dovie will get into her cage, yes. Ah, if I could just nestle down with her. But there *is* some bait that human beings jump for, after all, and it's called *money!* If she should want some of that, for instance? Eh, so what? I won't begrudge anything I have, naturally. How much can I give? Only a token, at most. And how to afford the gift for lifting her veil? Don't worry, my boy, it's easy enough. I'll present her with a few verses like these, and that takes care of it . . . . (Recites)

Thou, a dove thou art,
* just right for me,*
If I build a nest,
* my breast will agree.*
With both soul and heart
* I fell in love with thee.*
If I build a nest,
* my breast will agree.*

A penniless poet like me can't offer more for lifting her veil.
(Begins to sing the poem he has just recited.)

FOURTH SCENE   *MR. ARDENT-HACK, DAME BELLE,*
                     MRS. ACNE, MISS PLACID

DAME BELLE
My boy, Mrs. Acne and I have brought the bride. Come, take
her arm. Lead her to the seat of honor.

MR. ARDENT-HACK
(Gaily, clowning a little, comes to welcome the veiled Miss
Placid, escorted by Mrs. Acne) OOOHHH . . . .

DAME BELLE
(To Mrs. Acne) Friends, as soon as the new groom saw the
bride, he swooned with delight!

MR. ARDENT-HACK
No, no! *Not* swooned with delight! Perished from *shock*!

MRS. ACNE
(To Dame Belle) Oh my! the poor bride is starting to tremble.
Good lord, could she be getting feverish? (Seats Miss Placid in a
chair)

MR. ARDENT-HACK
(Pointing to Miss Placid) What is that?

DAME BELLE
That's Miss Placid, your beloved soulmate. She'll be your part-

16

SONG

(MR. ARDENT-HACK)

Thou, a dove thou art ————————

Just right for me ————————

If I build a nest ——— my breast will a—gree

Ah, my lit-tle bird ah, my lit-tle bird—

With both soul and heart — with both soul and heart

I fell in love with thee ———

17

If I build a nest —— my breast will a——gree

Ah, my lit-tle bird   ah, my lit-tle bird

The above melody is in a key suitable for a female voice. It can be dropped an octave or transposed to a lower range suitable for a male voice.

ner as long as you live.

MR. ARDENT-HACK
Partner for life? Spare me that pleasure! Let my soul quickly depart!

DAME BELLE
(To Mrs. Acne) Folks, the groom is deliriously happy. He's beside himself with joy!

MRS. ACNE
(To Dame Belle) The dear lad is in rapture because he's found his dream girl.

MR. ARDENT-HACK
(Anguished) Oh! Oh! Oh!

DAME BELLE
Let's not shed tears. You should laugh, make your enemies cry!

MR. ARDENT-HACK
Oh, if they knew the fix I'm in, how they'd roar!

DAME BELLE
Come on my lamb, raise the bride's veil and take a look at her face! Let your spirits soar!

MR. ARDENT-HACK
Soar! The instant I see her face, my heart will crash.

DAME BELLE
Lift her veil, my boy, lift it up! Remove any doubt that she's your sweetheart. (She and Mrs. Acne push Mr. Ardent-Hack to grasp Miss Placid's veil)

MR. ARDENT-HACK
I don't want to. (As he draws his hand back, it inadvertently catches Miss Placid's wig and pulls off both veil and wig, revealing her mature face and gray hair) WHAT is going on here??

DAME BELLE
EEEK! He's pulled the dear girl's hair right out by its platinum-blond roots!

MR. ARDENT-HACK

What's left there is plenty silvery, all right. See how brightly her own hair gleams!

DAME BELLE

Look here, you can't talk this way to her! That's for matron of honor and me. I'll teach you a lesson for insulting people. (To Mrs. Acne) Come on, Matron of Honor, take the bride outside at once! Send for the official who arranged the marriage contract! He's in the coffee shop next door. Have him round up the neighborhood crowd there and come on over. They'll straighten this fellow out!

FIFTH SCENE   *MR. ARDENT-HACK, DAME BELLE*

MR. ARDENT-HACK

D'you think the neighborhood mob will force me into marriage?

DAME BELLE

Marriage or jail—

MR. ARDENT-HACK

Rather than sleep in the same house with a wife like that, I'd much rather sleep in jail with peace of mind!

DAME BELLE

Just try jail for a while! See how you'll suffer, thanks to the torments you're causing me!

MR. ARDENT-HACK

Never fear, I owe so much money, thanks to you, that my creditors' prayers will keep me alive and well!

DAME BELLE

Oh yes? What if you should get sick?

MR. ARDENT-HACK

Do you imagine that my creditors won't send a doctor to cure me?

20

III.
MIDDLE-CLASS WOMEN OF CONSTANTINOPLE (unveiled
on the Left, veiled on the Right).

DAME BELLE

If they don't, what can you possibly do?

MR. ARDENT-HACK

I can really harm them terribly, after all.

DAME BELLE

And how, may I ask?

MR. ARDENT-HACK

By God, I'll up and die, just to spite them!

SIXTH SCENE   MR. ARDENT-HACK, DAME BELLE, MAS-
TER WISE, REVEREND GOBBLEDEGOOK, OFFICER
BOGGYWITS, NEIGHBORHOOD CROWD

REV. GOBBLEDEGOOK

(Bandana on his head, clothes awry, his speech crackling with
jerky glottal stops and "k" sounds pronounced far back in
the mouth) Does it make sense to rouse a person and rush him
over this way? Look how I'm dressed! Like a character in a
mummers' parade. Shame on you! What's this commotion all
about?

DAME BELLE

(Covering her head with the front of her smock, she humbly
kisses Rev. Gobbledegook's hand) Alas, my dear Reverend,
this scoundrel, the bridegroom-to-be, no longer wants the
woman he was yearning for. He tore every hair out of her head
. . .by the roots.   Not only that, he hasn't missed a single
chance to say nasty things to Matron of Honor and me. I'm
ashamed to repeat any of them to you.

REV. GOBBLEDEGOOK

(To Mr. Ardent-Hack) Oh, infamous wretch, oh, you . . . you—

MR. ARDENT-HACK

Reverend Gobbledegook, Your Honor, with your permission,
please. Let your humble servant explain the truth, as he sees

it!

REV. GOBBLEDEGOOK
Silence, lewd fellow! Would this poor woman, who is old enough to be your grandma, *prevaricate*?!?

DAME BELLE
Sir, he positively must marry this girl.

REV. GOBBLEDEGOOK
He must indeed! If he doesn't wed according to contract, he will have dishonored her. (To Neighborhood Crowd) Isn't that so, Neighbors?

NEIGHBORHOOD CROWD
You're right! You're right!

MR. ARDENT-HACK
I can't marry her, Your Honor. Something's wrong here. The girl you legally engaged me to is this one's little sister. I want that one!

REV. GOBBLEDEGOOK
No, I engaged you to the big sister.

MR. ARDENT-HACK
You did not!

REV. GOBBLEDEGOOK
Oh, I'm a liar, now, am I? What impertinence!

OFFICER BOGGYWITS
Sir, I got lots more dirt about this guy. I study 'im, y' know what ah mean? Listen, le' me tell y' right off. When I make th' rounds nights patrolin' th' precinct, I'm runnin' smack inna this mister big alla time. Out inna middle a th' street. Once't I up 'n ask "Where'dja come from?" He gimme some nice backtalk. What 'dye know, don' th' fool say: "I'm comin' from thi-ya-tor." Now that's nothin' but makin' a buffoon outa me, ain't it?

MR. ARDENT-HACK
Good Lord, what a studious fellow!

OFFICER BOGGYWITS
A stud you is, y'self, filthy nag! Don' keep talkin' dirty t' me, or I'll learn y' right now not t' snort an' sniff.

REV. GOBBLEDEGOOK
Officer Boggywits, this upstart is insolent and demented, too!

OFFICER BOGGYWITS
Th' way I see 't, he otta be tossed in th' clink and th' nut-house, both!

REV. GOBBLEDEGOOK
If you desire my counsel, we first have to obtain a document that certifies to his public insolence. We musn't let him stay in the precinct another minute. We don't want him around any longer.

NEIGHBORHOOD CROWD
We don't want him!

SEVENTH SCENE   MR. ARDENT HACK, DAME BELLE MRS. ACNE, REVEREND GOBBLEDEGOOK, OFFICER BOGGYWITS, RED SPARSEWHISKER, MASTER WISE, NEIGHBORHOOD CROWD

RED SPARSEWHISKER
(A tall basket on his back, oar-like paddle scoop in one hand and broom in the other) We don't want—

MASTER WISE
(Arriving just behind Red Sparsewhisker) What don't you want?

RED SPARSEWHISKER
How do I know? When the neighborhood folks say: "We don't want," I say the same. Whatever they say, it's got to be right.

MASTER WISE
Oh, and why are your neighbors right?

RED SPARSEWHISKER

Everybody knows good and . . . well, they're right, see? But how come, I can't say, exactly.

MASTER WISE

Then why stick your oar into something you don't know about?

RED SPARSEWHISKER

Oh, why not stick my oar in it? Aren't I one of the finest people in this precinct?

MASTER WISE

Just who are you?

RED SPARSEWHISKER

You say you don't recognize me? Red Sparsewhisker?

MASTER WISE

No.

RED SPARSEWHISKER

So, why're you prying into what's none of your business? Wise up, dummy, wise up! Have I got to explain everything to you? I'm a tenant in the precinct over there and "san-i-ta-tion man," they call it, in this one here.

MASTER WISE

Wake up, Mr. San-i-ty, wake up!

RED SPARSEWHISKER

You'd be as silly as I am, if you had any sense. Nothing's wrong with that! Better get moving, clear out, now!

REV. GOBBLEDEGOOK

(Pointing to Mr. Ardent-Hack and speaking to Master Wise) Oh, you're standing up for a reprobate like this, are you? Approving a sin is a sin in itself. You deserve punishment as much as he does.

MASTER WISE

My dear Reverend, don't get upset. (Surreptitiously showing a money bag) We want the little sister from you.

OFFICER BOGGYWITS
What's this, Boss? Is he tryin' t' grease y'r palm?

REV. GOBBLEDEGOOK
(To Officer Boggywits, stepping between him and Master Wise)
Would I take such a thing? None of that for me! (Aside to
Master Wise) Slip it into my side pocket! (Master Wise puts the
bag in Rev. Gobbledegook's side pocket)

RED SPARSEWHISKER
Did I hear you whisper, "Slip it in my side pocket?"

REV. GOBBLEDEGOOK
Of course not! I was saying, "Step aside! Stop it!" Who could
suspect me of anything?

OFFICER BOGGYWITS
Y' look pretty much like some bird what got a little . . .
baksheesh.

REV. GOBBLEDEGOOK
God forbid! God forbid! May my hands wither up if they've
so much as touched money.

MASTER WISE
Pardon me, Your Honor, whatever the truth may be, bring it
right out in the open. Proceed as befits a man of your standing.

REV. GOBBLEDEGOOK
You have expressed your wish most nobly. So, rage has left
my heart and compassion has taken its place. (To Neighborhood Crowd) Attention, everybody! I begin to see another
sort of justice in this case. In fact, I suddenly remembered
something.

NEIGHBORHOOD CROWD
What's that?

REV. GOBBLEDEGOOK
You know, a little while ago I stated that the Miss whose
marriage agreement I had sealed was the big sister. Now, when
I said "big" sister, I didn't mean big in age, but big in size. The

older sister is past forty. She is no match for the honorable bridegroom. There now! That is all I know. Anyplace, anytime, I shall testify honestly, just like this.

OFFICER BOGGYWITS
'Cause y've d'clared everthin' so sincere, we'll go along with 't, alla way.

NEIGHBORHOOD CROWD
Right! Right!

REV. GOBBLEDEGOOK
(To Mrs. Acne) Matron of Honor, go get the real bride! Make sure she is the one who is tall in size but small in years! Let me give her away to the bridegroom with my own hand. No more mistakes! (To Master Wise) If there have been any other slip-ups, say so! I shall straighten them out impartially, also. I am proud to perform such friendly service.

OFFICER BOGGYWITS
(To Mr. Ardent-Hack) Boss, any little tings I said t' y' a while ago was just f'r fun. I was hopin' t' make y' laugh, and t' jolly y' up when y' was blue.

RED SPARSEWHISKER
(To Master Wise) Good gentleman, if I ever poke my oar again into anything except the neighborhood trash, I am not worthy of a *san-i-ta-tion* man's job!

EIGHTH SCENE   MR. ARDENT-HACK, MASTER WISE, DAME BELLE, MRS. ACNE, MISS DOVE, REVEREND GOBBLEDEGOOK, OFFICER BOGGYWITS, RED SPARSE-WHISKER, NEIGHBORHOOD CROWD

MRS. ACNE
(Brings in Miss Dove, who is apparently crying and rubbing her eyes one minute and covering her face the next with one hand and peering sideways through her fingers at Mr. Ardent-Hack) There, kind Sir! The true bride!

REV. GOBBLEDEGOOK

(To Mrs. Acne) Why is she crying? Doesn't she want our bridegroom, after all?

MRS. ACNE

(After whispering quietly with Miss Dove) Your Honor? I asked why she was crying, and I understand it, a tiny bit. But, I guess it's not what you think, though.

REV. GOBBLEDEGOOK

Well, what is it?

MRS. ACNE

(Sigh) The poor, sad, little doll! Earlier, she was so miserable she cried and cried because she couldn't have this groom. Now, maybe she's sorry for wasting all those tears. . . so, she's weeping for all that waste!

REV. GOBBLEDEGOOK

(To Miss Dove, very gently) When I hear you sobbing like that, my heart throbs with such feeling that I'm almost ready to serve as your matron of honor myself. (Making Miss Dove and Mr. Ardent-Hack join hands) Take her, my dear poet. From now on, see that you find a way of making her smile. From the bottom of my heart I pray that you live in harmony. (To Master Wise) Is there anything else I can do for you?

MASTER WISE

Yes. Take everyone out of the house with you . . . except the bride and groom, I beg you.

REV. GOBBLEDEGOOK

Why beg? Command, my Effendi! (To Neighborhood Crowd) Here we go, folks! (To Dame Belle) Let's go, Madam Matchmaker! (To Mrs. Acne) Let's go, Matron of Honor!

NINTH SCENE   *MR. ARDENT-HACK, MASTER WISE*
                      MISS DOVE

MR. ARDENT-HACK

(Takes Miss Dove by the arm, and together—with sidelong glances—they coquettishly admire one another. He turns to Master Wise) Oh, aren't you leaving with the neighbors? You still have something left to do here?

MASTER WISE
Only to impart a word or two of wisdom.

MR. ARDENT-HACK
Dear Man, please come tomorrow and share a thousand or two of them with me. See how closely I shall listen, then.

MASTER WISE
Certainly not. Now is the time to share them.

MR. ARDENT-HACK
If you really must! But, hurry it up! (Turning his head toward Miss Dove, he pays no attention to Master Wise's chatter)

MASTER WISE
So, my beloved friend!

MR. ARDENT-HACK
Isn't it finished yet?

MASTER WISE
Hold on, Sir! I haven't started yet!

MR. ARDENT-HACK
It's dragged out so!

MASTER WISE
Don't you regret getting married without consulting a friend like me?

MR. ARDENT-HACK
Come on, are you trying to make me confess my sins, or what?

MASTER WISE
Look, this is the kind of mess people get into when they rely on matchmakers. The nerve of those people, to act as brokers of love and affection for their own personal gain!

MR. ARDENT-HACK

(Sigh) Look here, pal, I'm afraid you're going to be awfully late to wherever it is you're going. I musn't let you fall behind in your work this way.

MASTER WISE

See what obstacles you and your wife ran up against, trying to get married. And you already knew each other quite well!

MR. ARDENT-HACK

Even before the wedding, I wanted to have a dream that could foretell events. Somehow, that idea must have gotten lost. Now, if you'll forgive me, let me go and dream, while it's on my mind. After that, *you* will have to come and interpret the visions I see.

MASTER WISE

Draw the obvious conclusions about couples who are wedded without ever knowing each other in the least! What will their plight be, if . . . .

MR. ARDENT-HACK

(Rubbing his eyes) Uh! All this good advice has tired me so, I'm dying to sleep. With your blessing, may I go and take a short nap?

MASTER WISE

Very well, I'm leaving. Go ahead! Do whatever you wish from now on. But . . . remember the lesson you learned, you hear?

MR. ARDENT-HACK

Don't worry. How can I ever forget it? I nearly ruined myself before I finally mastered the theory of marriage. (Putting his arm around Miss Dove's waist) Now, I don't expect to make the slightest mistake putting it correctly into practice.

C U R T A I N

COUNCIL on NATIONAL LITERATURES

BOOKS

PROBLEMS IN NATIONAL LITERARY IDENTITY AND THE WRITER AS SOCIAL CRITIC

EDITED BY
ANNE PAOLUCCI

WITH A PREFACE BY
DONALD PUCHALA
Associate Dean, School of International
Affairs, Columbia University

AND

THE ANNUAL SILVER LECTURE BY
SALIM AHMED SALIM
Permanent Representative of the United
Republic of Tanzania to the United Nations

SELECTED PAPERS OF THE FOURTH ANNUAL NDEA
SEMINAR ON FOREIGN AREA STUDIES
COLUMBIA UNIVERSITY, FEBRUARY 28-29, 1980

PAPERS BY: *Robert Black (Council on Learning), Elena Klepikova (Russian Institute, Columbia University), Robin Lewis (Department of English, Columbia University), Bernth Lindfors (Ed.* Research in African Literatures, *University of Texas/Austin), Anne Paolucci (Executive Director, Council on National Literatures), Frank J. Warnke (Ch. Comparative Literature Department, University of Georgia/Athens)*

ISBN:0-918680-11-5 LCCC:80-83126 GHSS901/$5.95 (+$1. p/h)
[ALL ORDERS ARE PREPAID; US $ ONLY]